GROUNDBREAKERS

Alexander Fleming

Steve Parker

Heinemann Library
Chicago, Illinois

© 2001 Reed Educational & Professional Publishing
Published by Heinemann Library,
an imprint of Reed Educational & Professional Publishing,
Chicago, IL
Customer Service 888-454-2279

Visit our website at www.heinemannlibrary.com

Designed by Katrina ffiske
Illustrated by Michael Posen
Originated by Ambassador Litho
Printed in Hong Kong

05 04 03 02
10 9 8 7 6 5 4 3

Library of Congress Cataloging-in-Publication
Parker, Steve.
   Alexander Fleming / Steve Parker.
     p. cm. -- (Groundbreakers)
   Includes bibliographical references and index.
   ISBN 1-58810-050-2 (library)
    1. Fleming, Alexander, 1881-1955--Juvenile literature. 2. Bacteriologists--Great
Britain--Biography--Juvenile literature. 3. Penicillin--History--Juvenile literature. [1.
Fleming, Alexander, 1881-1955. 2. Scientists. 3. Penicilin--History.] I. Title. II. Series.

QR31.F5 P37 2001
616'.014'092--dc21
[B]

00-063267

Acknowledgments
The author and publishers are grateful to the following for permission to reproduce copyright material: AKG
London, pp. 10, 32; Art Archive, p. 9; Corbis/East Ayrshire Museum and Arts Council, p. 7; Dr. Robert Fleming, p. 24;
Hulton Getty, p. 27; Imperial War Museum, p. 23; London Scottish Regimental Trust, p. 11; Cordelia Molloy, p. 43; Mary
Evans Picture Library, pp. 8, 17, 20; MPM Images, pp. 25, 33; Musée de Versailles/Dagli Orti, pp. 19, 37; Popperfoto, pp. 22, 40,
41; Science and Society Picture Library pp. 4, 12. Science Museum, pp. 18, 28, 36, 39; Science Photo Library, p. 5; Science
Photo Library/Dr. Jeremy Burgess, pp. 30, 31; Science Photo Library,/ St. Mary's Hospital Medical School, p. 14; Science
Photo Library,/St. Mary's Hospital Medical School, p. 15; Science Photo Library/St. Mary's Hospital Medical School, p. 16;
Science Photo Library/St. Mary's Hospital Medical School, p. 29; Science Photo Library,/Geoff Tompkinson, p. 13; Secchi-
Lecaque/Roussel-UCLA, pp. 34, 42.

Cover photograph reproduced with the permission of Popperfoto.

Some words are shown in bold, **like this.** You can find out what they mean by looking in the glossary.

Contents

The Man Who Saved Millions

Every day around the world, millions of people have medical operations, or surgery. During or after surgery, it is possible for tiny living things, known as germs, to get into the body through the surgical cut, or incision, and multiply. The germs can cause an **infection.** Infection can also happen after an accident, when the skin is broken by a cut or wound and gets dirty.

From the mid-1940s, Alexander Fleming, with his trademark bow tie, was known around the world as one of the first "medical superstars."

The terrible risk of infection

Today, the risks of infection are tiny. But about 60 years ago, they were very serious. Surgery was used much less often in those days, because people were generally less likely to get better after the operation and more likely to die from infection. In wars and conflicts, more soldiers died from infection of their injuries and wounds than died from the actual injuries themselves.

A chance discovery

Born in 1881 in Scotland, Alexander Fleming was one of the scientists who helped to end this problem. In 1928, he made one of the greatest discoveries in all of medicine, while working at St. Mary's Hospital in London. Almost by accident, Fleming found a mysterious substance that killed **microscopic** germs, especially the types of germs known as **bacteria,** that can cause many different kinds of infections. The substance was made by a type of natural mold or fungus that grew as a fluffy layer on rotting fruit, soil, and other items.

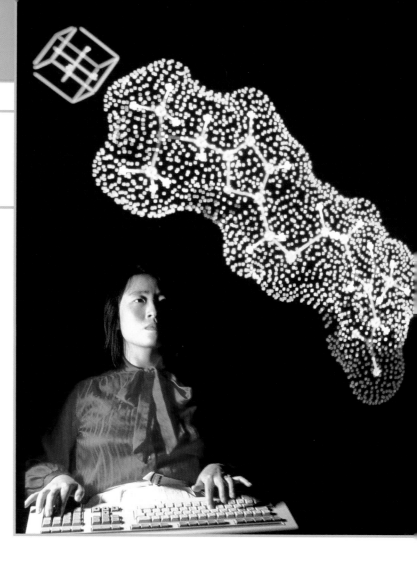

A researcher today uses a computer to work on models of the structures of possible new drugs.

Worldwide fame

At the time, Fleming's marvelous discovery did not make world headlines. But through a series of chance events, other scientists began to work on the mysterious mold-produced substance. They made it pure, tested it, and showed that it was indeed an amazingly powerful germ-killer. Toward the end of World War II (1939–45), the drug was mass-produced and used to treat wounded soldiers, with incredible success. Fleming's chance discovery really did save millions of lives, and it has been doing so ever since.

This mysterious substance is **penicillin.** Its success made Alexander Fleming one of the most famous people in the world. He has been remembered by almost every nation on Earth. Even the moon has a crater named after him.

ONGOING IMPACT   A new era in medicine

Penicillin is an **antibiotic** drug. Antibiotics harm or kill the types of germs known as bacteria. Since Fleming's time, many more antibiotics, now numbering more than 8,000, have been discovered to treat many different kinds of infections. They have changed medicine so much that doctors speak of the "pre-antibiotic era." Before penicillin, infection was such a great and ever-present threat that it was one of the biggest killers. We live in the "antibiotic era," when infection is less likely, and medicine is much safer.

Small Beginnings

Alexander Fleming was born on August 6, 1881, at Lochfield, a hill farm in rugged moorland country near the town of Darvel, in Ayrshire county, Scotland. His father, Hugh, ran the farm. Hugh Fleming had four children—Jane, Hugh, Tom, and Mary—by his first wife, who had died in 1874. Two years later, Hugh married Grace Morton. Together, they had four more children—Grace, John, Alexander, and Robert.

When Alec was growing up, children had to entertain themselves. This photograph from that period shows boys who have been fishing in their local river.

Alexander was small for his age, and was known as "Little Alec." His main childhood friend was his younger brother, Robert. The whole family helped on their farm, where they raised sheep and cows, and grew hay and wheat.

Life on the farm

Lochfield was about four miles (six kilometers) across steep countryside from the nearest town, Darvel. There were no cars, no radio, and no television when the Fleming children were growing up. In summer, the youngsters played outdoors, catching trout in the streams and rabbits on the moors. "Little Alec" soon showed that he was an excellent wildlife observer. He was also skilled with his hands, able to grab trout straight from the water. In winter, the brothers and sisters made their own entertainment. Alec enjoyed making new toys and playing funny games. His powers of memory and observation, and his ability to make things, would be useful in the future.

This was Lochfield Farm, Alec's birthplace and childhood home, in the 1970s. The Flemings rented the farm from the Earl of Loudoun.

Off to school

Alec attended the nearby village primary school, called Loudoun Moor. There were only twelve to fifteen pupils, mostly from two or three local families. Alec was clever, and he did well at school without working too hard.

In 1888, when Alec was seven, his father died from a short illness at the age of 72. Alec's oldest half brother, Hugh, who was 24 years old, took over the running of the farm. In 1891, Alec moved on to the secondary school at Darvel. Every day, he made the long walk of several miles there and back. Although he was small for his age, Alec grew strong and sturdy. At Darvel school, he again made good grades. In a playground accident at Darvel, Alec broke his nose as he went around a corner and crashed into another boy.

In 1893, Alec left school at Darvel to attend a secondary school, Kilmarnock Academy. The large, busy town of Kilmarnock was about 16 miles (26 kilometers) from Alec's home in Lochfield. Alec stayed in Kilmarnock during the week with his aunt, and traveled home by train and horse-drawn carriage for weekends. Sometimes, he missed the carriage and had to walk the last six miles (about ten kilometers) to Lochfield. Again, at Kilmarnock he did well in school and made many friends.

A Move to London

At the beginning of the twentieth century, motor vehicles were beginning to crowd the streets of London, but there were still many horse-drawn carriages.

Alec's oldest half brother, Hugh, ran the farm at Lochfield, but he could not support the growing family. Local jobs were hard to find. Alec's second-oldest half brother, Tom, had trained to become a doctor and moved to London. Tom set up as an **oculist** at 144 Marylebone Road, examining people's eyes and prescribing glasses. Their sister Mary went along as housekeeper. In 1893, Tom suggested that his half brother John should also move to London and become an apprentice lens maker. The business began to prosper. In 1895, Tom asked Alec if he would like to come to London, with its great opportunities for study and work. Alec was not quite fourteen years old when he left Kilmarnock Academy and moved south. Six months later, Robert joined them, so there were four brothers and one sister in London.

Learning to keep quiet

In remote Scotland, the Flemings had always been a close family, and supported each other. They were the same in bustling London. Alec and Robert went to the Regent Street Polytechnic School to continue their studies. Their Scottish education was ahead of English teaching, and Alec moved up two classes in two weeks to be with much bigger, older boys. At first, they laughed at Alec's strong Scottish accent, outdated clothes, and what they saw as his strange manners. Alec quickly learned to speak only when necessary. However, the two Fleming brothers' quiet intelligence, helpfulness, and sense of fun gradually won over their classmates.

Life in London

Alec and Robert walked for hours looking at the fashionable people and great sights of the city. They also rode on the new steam-powered Underground Railway. The brothers were impressed with the new technology in the city, but were saddened to see the poverty and disease in London's slums.

In the 1860s, Louis Pasteur's scientific skills helped to save the French wine industry from collapse.

DEATH OF A HERO

The year Alec moved to London, the great French scientist Louis Pasteur (1822–1895) died. Pasteur had shown that beer and wine went "bad" because **microscopic** living things from the air landed in them and multiplied. In medicine, he made **vaccines** to protect against dreaded diseases such as **rabies.** At school, Alec had read about Pasteur's great achievements. Pasteur would become one of Alec's heroes, and later, Alec's own work would be based on germs and disease.

The Young Fleming

Tom Fleming became a successful medical **oculist,** and the family moved to a larger house at 29 York Street, just off Baker Street in London. Mary got married and moved out, but Alec's sister Grace came down from Lochfield to take over the housekeeping duties. After two years at the Regent Street Polytechnic School, it was time for Alec to find a job.

Alec was interested in many things, but could not decide what he wanted to do for work. In 1897, he drifted into a job as office clerk for the America Line, a shipping company in London. Alec's work involved filing and keeping the shipping company's records up to date. It was not a very interesting job, but he worked hard and stayed there for four years.

In the army

At the end of 1899, the Boer War broke out in South Africa. In Britain, young men were urged to join the armed forces. Loyal to their country, Alec and his brother John signed up in 1900 as privates, or low-ranking soldiers, in the London Scottish Rifle Volunteers.

These British troops ride into battle in the Boer War. Alec joined the army when the war broke out.

Robert followed them a few months later, as soon as he turned eighteen. None of the Flemings saw war action or even went overseas, but they trained hard with their regiment, mainly part-time, in evenings and weekends. After their childhood on the Scottish hills, the brothers coped easily with the long marches. Alec's helpful nature showed on a long train trip to Edinburgh. The carriage was so crowded that he, as the smallest soldier, volunteered to lie in the luggage rack the entire way.

In the army, Alec quickly discovered that his fitness, strength, powers of concentration, sharp eyes, and steady, skilled hands made him a fine sportsman. He learned to swim, joined the water polo team, won awards for rifle-shooting, and took up golf. He remained a private in the London Scottish Rifle Volunteers for fourteen years, leaving only when his scientific work became too time-consuming.

This magazine cover shows the London Scottish Regiment, with Alec among them, marching to a 1908 rifle-shooting competition.

THE BOER WAR

The Boer War lasted from 1899 to 1902. The war was between two sets of European settlers in South Africa, over land and mineral resources, such as gold. The Boers, or Afrikaners, in the regions of Orange Free State and Transvaal, had Dutch ancestors. The British settlers and rulers occupied the neighboring Cape colony. During the war, thousands of soldiers arrived back in England, dead or dying from wounds and **infections.** The conflict was headline news, and many people, including Alec, hoped for better medical treatment.

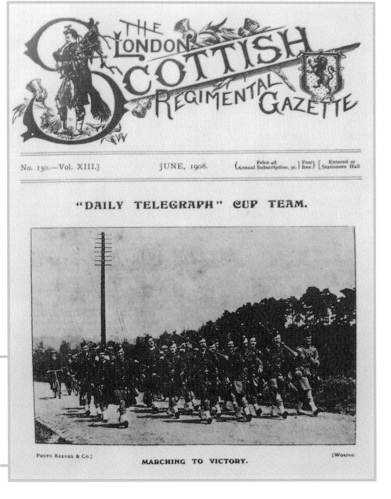

THE LONDON SCOTTISH REGIMENTAL GAZETTE

No. 150.—Vol. XIII.]   JUNE, 1908.   (Price 4d. Annual Subscription, 5s.) [Post free] [Entered at Stationers' Hall

"DAILY TELEGRAPH" CUP TEAM.

PHOTO KEENES & CO.]   MARCHING TO VICTORY.   [WOKING

A Medical Student

In Fleming's words:

Alec often spoke about medicine as teamwork and compared it to team sports such as water polo. In later years, he told an audience of medical students:

"There are some people who think that medical students should spend all their time learning medicine and give up games. I don't agree…. There is far more in medicine than mere book work. You have to know human nature. There is no better way to learn about human nature than by indulging in sports, more especially in team sports."

In 1901, the Fleming children each inherited a large sum of money after the death of an aged uncle, John Fleming, back in Darvel. This was one of many chance events which had a great effect on Alec's life. He talked to his brother Tom about what to do with the money. Tom suggested that Alec could put his inheritance toward training for a new career—perhaps medicine.

Passing exams

Alec gave up his office job. Before he could become a medical student, he had to pass exams to get in to the medical schools where doctors were trained. So he went to the London College of **Preceptors** for more classes. Once again, his grades were good, especially in English and the general knowledge exam. Alec also took exams in other subjects, including algebra, English history, geography, arithmetic, geometry, French, Latin, and scripture. He seemed to have the gift of predicting exam questions. He tried to think like a teacher, deciding which topics would make good questions, and concentrating his studies on these. This cut down his work—and luckily for him, he was usually correct.

Operating rooms looked like this at the time that Alec was studying medicine.

To St. Mary's

Alec now had to choose a medical school. He remembered that he had played water polo against a team from St. Mary's Hospital when he was in the army. This hospital was in Paddington, London, within walking distance of his York Street home, so it was convenient for Alec to study there. In October 1901, he became a medical student at the medical school attached to St. Mary's Hospital. Alec's association with St. Mary's would last for more than 50 years.

At last, Alec had found a subject that interested him greatly. The idea of being a doctor fit with his caring, helpful nature. He studied hard, and excelled at his medical exams. He usually came in first or second, trading places with a fellow student, C. A. Pannett. Between them, they won most of St. Mary's medals, prizes, and awards. Pannett eventually became a leading surgeon, and he and Alec remained lifelong friends.

Joining the Team

Alec worked in the Inoculation Department of St. Mary's Hospital.

In 1903, Alec's mother, Grace, followed her sons and daughter and moved from Lochfield to London. Alec, John, and Robert moved to live with her at a house in Ealing, West London.

The following year, Alec began to think about his medical specialty, or what kind of doctor he wanted to become. He liked anatomy, the study of the parts and structure of the body, and his skilled hands made him exceptional at surgical operations. So in 1905, he took the first in a series of exams to join the **Royal College of Surgeons.** As usual, he passed easily. The following summer, Alec passed his main exams to become a qualified doctor and a member of the Royal College of Surgeons (MRCS). He still needed some of his surgical qualifications, but he needed a job to earn money while he studied. He considered moving to another London hospital. But once again a chance event cropped up that would affect the rest of his life.

A new job

Alec was an important member of St. Mary's rifle-shooting team. So was another doctor and researcher at St. Mary's, John Freeman. He knew that if Alec left for another hospital, then the team would have less chance of winning an important cup that year. Freeman worked in the **Inoculation** Department of St. Mary's, where new **vaccines** were made and tested. There was an opening available for a junior assistant.

Here was a way to keep Fleming at St. Mary's and on the rifle team. Freeman spoke to the head of the department, and in late summer 1906, Alec took the job of junior assistant.

The big boss

Almroth Wright was the head of the Inoculation Department at St. Mary's. He was a larger-than-life character in almost every way. In the year Fleming joined his department, Wright was knighted to become Sir Almroth Wright. He was also made a **fellow** of the **Royal Society,** a great honor for any scientist. Wright had an enormous and lasting effect on Fleming's life and career. The two would become great friends, although there would be many disputes along the way.

SIR ALMROTH WRIGHT (1861–1947)

Almroth Wright was one of the most famous medical people of his time. He was a strong supporter of using inoculation to help the body's natural defenses fight disease. He talked and wrote not only about medical topics such as the causes of disease and the need for inoculation, but about other great debates of the day, such as the role of royalty and whether women should be allowed to vote. He wrote many scientific and medical articles and also sent strongly worded letters to the newspapers. Wright inspired respect—and occasionally fear—in his colleagues.

Almroth Wright was head of the Inoculation Department at the time Alec started work there.

The Challenges of Medicine

As Fleming began his work in the **Inoculation** Department of St. Mary's Hospital in 1906, hospitals and medicine were very different compared to today. One of the greatest problems was **infection** by germs, especially **microscopic bacteria.** Today, it is difficult for us to imagine that infection was once so common and serious. But in Fleming's time, it killed thousands of people every week.

The problem of infection

A small cut or scratch might become a breeding ground for germs. These could quickly spread through the body and even threaten a person's life. Infection was a serious risk of surgery, too. Thanks to the pioneering work of Joseph Lister, **antiseptics** had been in use since the 1860s. They killed some of the germs on surgical tools like scissors and scalpel blades, on the bandages and other dressings used for patients, and also in the cuts, or incisions, that the surgeon made in the body. But infection was still a serious threat, especially in the first few days following an operation.

Growing germs

Fleming's work involved studying samples of blood, pus, and other substances taken from patients. He would look through a microscope at the samples and see what bacteria and other germs they contained. He would then add smears of the samples to a substance called **culture medium.** This encouraged the germs to grow and multiply. The culture medium might be a liquid in a flask, or a jelly-like layer in a special small, shallow dish with a lid, called a petri dish.

Joseph Lister was one of the first surgeons to use antiseptics, starting in the mid-1860s. Before his time, most doctors did not even understand the need for clean hands during surgery.

Elie Metchnikoff observed microscopic body cells surrounding and eating bacteria, as part of the body's defense against infection.

Different culture media containing slightly different ingredients encouraged different bacteria and other germs to grow. The individual bacteria were far too small to see. But as they multiplied into thousands and millions in the petri dish, they could be seen as small, round, colored patches on the surface of the jelly. These patches were bacterial **colonies.** Fleming examined the colonies to find the exact identity of the bacteria, how they lived, and how they might be killed in the fight against infection.

ONGOING IMPACT   Medical progress

In Fleming's time, some of the recent advances in medicine included:

- development of the rabies **vaccine** by Louis Pasteur
- the use of germ-killing substances, called antiseptics, during operations. English surgeon Joseph Lister (1827–1912) pioneered the use of antiseptics.
- identifying bacteria by coloring or staining them with special chemicals, and showing which ones caused which diseases. The founder of this work was German researcher Robert Koch (1843–1910).
- the discovery that, in the human body, some microscopic cells called white blood cells "eat" invading germs. This process, called **phagocytosis,** is part of the body's fight against infection. It was discovered by Russian-French scientist Elie Metchnikoff (1845–1916).

The Inoculation Department

In 1906, Alec's mother moved to a new house at 125 Clarence Gate Gardens, near Regent's Park. Again, her sons moved with her. This house was conveniently close to St. Mary's Hospital, and Alec lived a settled life at home. He still attended occasional events with the London Scottish Rifle Volunteers, and enjoyed taking part in trivia games, golf, and table tennis matches, and playing sports and games with his brothers.

THE FIRST INOCULATION

Inoculation was first tested scientifically by English doctor Edward Jenner (1749–1823). He used it to protect people against the terrible disease of **smallpox,** in 1796. Smallpox inoculation became widespread after about 1850. By Fleming's time, there was active research into many kinds of vaccines against various diseases.

What is inoculation?

At St. Mary's, Alec continued his laboratory work in the **Inoculation** Department. Inoculation, or **vaccination,** involves giving someone a vaccine, usually by injection. The vaccine contains dead or weakened versions of the **bacterial** germs, or their products, that cause a disease. The body becomes protected or immune to the germs without suffering the disease. Vaccination is a routine process today, given to millions of people each year.

In the early 1900s, inoculation was the subject of great debate. Some doctors doubted it was effective. Almroth Wright was a strong supporter, and his department aimed to develop better, safer vaccines. The workers grew bacteria, killed or weakened them with chemicals, tested them, and sold the best vaccines to other hospitals and medical centers.

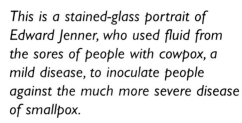

This is a stained-glass portrait of Edward Jenner, who used fluid from the sores of people with cowpox, a mild disease, to inoculate people against the much more severe disease of smallpox.

Fleming (in the white laboratory coat) stands with a group of colleagues from the Inoculation Department.

The career ladder

Alec was developing an interest in bacteria and vaccines, but he still hoped to become a surgeon. In 1908, he passed his final medical exams and earned his bachelor of medicine and surgery degree, winning the London University Gold Medal for his excellent grades. He also became a teacher, instructing St. Mary's medical students—a post he held until 1914—and he began to write medical and scientific articles. In 1908, he won a second gold medal for his detailed account of how bacteria cause sudden **infections,** *The Diagnosis of Acute Bacterial Infection.*

Also in 1908, Alec became a part-time surgeon at St. Mary's Hospital, carrying out small operations and helping with major ones. In the same year, his first reports and articles were published in the famous medical journals *The Lancet* and *The Practitioner.* Alec would write more than one hundred reports during his lifetime.

In 1909, Alec finally achieved one of the few definite goals he ever had. He became a **fellow,** or senior member, of the **Royal College of Surgeons** (FRCS). He was truly climbing the ladder of a successful career in medicine.

The "Magic Bullet"

Alec worked hard in the **Inoculation** Department, where he was known as "Little Flem." In 1909, he heard news of an important medical breakthrough. German medical scientist Paul Ehrlich (1854–1915), working in Frankfurt, had made a new kind of medical drug, called 606 or Salvarsan. It was the first major drug to be produced in a chemical laboratory rather than obtained from natural sources such as plants or animals. It was nicknamed the "magic bullet" because it killed certain invading **bacteria** in the body without harming the body's own cells and parts.

By this time, Fleming had another part-time job treating patients with **sexually transmitted diseases.** Salvarsan was effective against one of the diseases, **syphilis.** Fleming obtained supplies of the "magic bullet" and used it with great success. But this practice went against Almroth Wright's faith in helping the body to fight its own battles using natural substances, rather than laboratory-made chemicals. Wright and Fleming began to disagree about the direction that future medical research should take. Would they try to improve the body's natural resistance to disease, or fight disease with chemically produced drugs?

*Paul Ehrlich worked in many areas of medicine and helped to begin the science of immunology—the study of how the body protects itself against **microbes** and disease.*

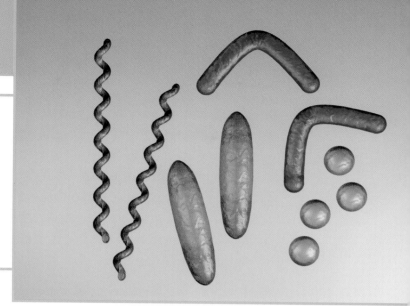

Alec worked on bacteria all his life. Under the microscope, the thousands of different types of bacteria can be recognized by to their shapes: spirilli (corkscrew-shaped), cocci (ball-shaped), bacilli (oval-shaped), and vibrio (comma- or V-shaped).

Life in the lab

The Inoculation Department at St. Mary's Hospital was a small collection of crowded laboratories and workrooms known as "the lab," where Almroth Wright was the undisputed boss. On a typical day, the staff arrived promptly at 9 A.M. Fleming would set off on his ward rounds, visiting patients in the hospital. He checked and examined them, and took samples of blood and saliva, pus from wounds, and scrapings of skin. In the afternoon, Alec grew bacteria in tubes and dishes and studied them under the microscope. Ever since he was a child, Alec had been good at making things. He soon became expert at making specialized new equipment, especially pieces of glassware such as test tubes. In the late afternoon, the lab staff assembled in their meeting room. Wright, seated in his large chair, made an opening remark about their research, or general medicine, or a piece of news. A lively discussion usually followed. Sometimes, Fleming and the others did not leave until after midnight.

Social life

At work, "Little Flem" was still quiet and shy, but away from work, he was widening his social life. Some of his patients were wealthy and powerful, and through them he developed new friendships with the artists Fred Pegram and Ronald Gray. They invited him to the Chelsea Arts Club, a popular meeting place for writers and artists. Alec greatly enjoyed their company. By about 1912, he was a regular visitor at the club, and he later became a member.

A SENSE OF FUN

Alec was usually quiet and serious, but he had a great sense of fun. In addition to making glass lab equipment, he also made beautiful glass toys such as cats and dogs. He grew bacteria on dishes, not for work, but to make pretty patterns with their shapes and colors. He called these his "germ paintings."

World War I

In 1914, the outbreak of World War I shattered the regular routine of London life. Almroth Wright, who had once been an army doctor, was appointed as a colonel in the Royal Army Medical Corps. He took his staff and equipment from the lab at St. Mary's and went to France. They set up a hospital in the Casino, a large building in the town of Boulogne, on the coast of northern France. "Little Flem," by now a senior and respected researcher, was appointed as Wright's lieutenant.

Earlier, Wright had strongly suggested that soldiers be **vaccinated** against **typhoid.** This practice saved thousands of lives, and its success greatly affected Alec. While in France, Alec began to think of staying in vaccine research rather than becoming a surgeon. He saw that battlefield injuries were still difficult to treat, especially wounds that got dirty in the mud of the trenches. The gigantic scale of the battles meant that tens of thousands of soldiers could be injured in one day, overwhelming the army's medical services. Soldiers often developed **infections** such as **septicemia, tetanus,** and **gangrene.** Even if skilled army surgeons could repair the wounds and injuries, infections usually claimed the soldiers' lives.

During World War I, thousands of soldiers died every day, often from infections rather than their actual wounds.

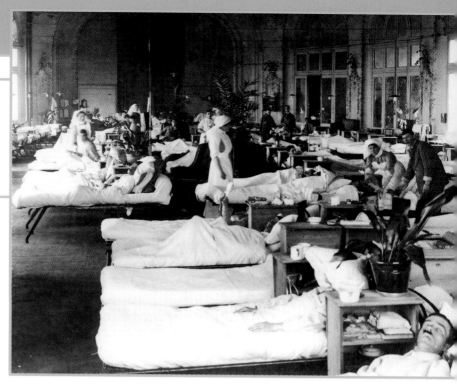

This large hall in France was converted to a military hospital for injured troops during World War I.

First-class research

By now, Fleming was becoming well known as a **bacteria** expert, or **bacteriologist.** While treating his soldier patients, he also carried out research on the bacteria in the soldiers' wounds. His idea was to see if **antiseptics,** widely used during operations to kill germs, really were effective. In a fine piece of medical research that Fleming carried out while treating soldiers at the Casino, he combined results from laboratory experiments with tests on real people. He showed that antiseptics used in certain ways did more harm than good. The antiseptics destroyed many of the bacteria, but they also killed off some of the body's own defenses, especially the white blood cells that "ate," or destroyed, germs. It was better in some cases to use antiseptics sparingly, and to encourage the body to fight its own battle against germs, just as Wright always insisted.

Fleming also improved methods for putting blood from donors into patients. This process, called blood **transfusion,** is common today, but it was new during World War I. Wright, Fleming, and the medical team at the Boulogne Casino had other successes, too. Fleming was promoted to captain and received glowing praise from his superiors.

A TIME OF PROGRESS

Medicine advanced quickly in the years during and soon after World War I. Blood transfusions became much safer, partly due to Alexander Fleming's work in France. **X-ray** equipment, invented in the 1890s, became more common and accurate. The bacteria that caused whooping cough were identified, and a **vaccine** was developed against **Rocky Mountain spotted fever.** However, there was still the enormous problem of infection by bacteria after surgical operations, or many kinds of accidental injuries.

23

A Devoted Couple

In 1915, while in the army, Alec went on leave from France, returned to London—and got married. It was a great surprise to almost everyone who knew him. His wife was Sarah "Sally" McElroy. Sally ran a nursing home in Baker Street with her twin sister, Elizabeth. This was near the Fleming family home in Clarence Gate Gardens. The Flemings and the McElroys had become friendly over the past year or so, and romance blossomed. Alec and Sally were married on December 23, 1915. Soon afterward, Alec's brother John married Elizabeth.

While Alec was quiet, shy, and sometimes awkward, Sally was lively, talkative, and confident. They were devoted to each other. After World War I, Alec returned to his job at the **Inoculation** Department of St. Mary's Hospital. He and Sally set up home in an apartment in Bickenhall Mansions, while John and Elizabeth stayed in the Clarence Gate Gardens home nearby.

The former "Little Flem" was now a senior medical researcher and leading expert on **bacteria.** In 1919, Wright appointed him assistant director of the Inoculation Department—second in charge. Alec's promotion meant more money, so he could afford to give up his part-time work treating patients to focus on his research. Sally sold her nursing home business. The Flemings now had more free time. Alec liked to stop in at the Chelsea Arts Club on most days after work, to meet friends and sometimes play a game, before returning home for the evening.

Alec and Sally were very happy together. They were married for almost thirty-four years. This picture shows them in 1944, on a visit to Belfast.

A country house

Alec and Sally often visited friends in the countryside. On a trip to Suffolk in 1921, they stayed with the Pegrams, Alec's friends from the

Chelsea Arts Club. The Flemings had become interested in antiques and went to see some items at an auction in a house called Penny Royal, in Barton Mills. They ended up buying the house itself. Sally and Alec changed its name to The Dhoon, and it became their country home. Sally often stayed and worked on the garden, while Alec returned on weekends and vacations. They invited many friends, and Alec loved to play croquet on the lawn and go fishing in the river, as he had done when he was a child.

ONGOING IMPACT) A new type of germ

In 1918, a serious form of the disease influenza, or flu, swept across the world, killing millions. Fleming tried to find the cause. But he could not link it to any bacteria. It is now known that flu is due to a **virus,** a type of germ far smaller than bacteria, and too small to see with the microscopes of Fleming's time. However, Fleming's results were useful because they helped to guide research work away from bacteria and toward finding this new type of germ.

The Puzzle of Lysozyme

In the early 1920s, St. Mary's Hospital received a large donation from the University Grants Committee, an organization that helped to fund new areas in medicine and surgery. Now that St. Mary's had this money to buy new equipment, it was time for reorganization. In 1921, the old **Inoculation** Department became the new **Pathology** and Research Department, with Wright at its head.

A germ-killer

At about this time, Fleming began to work on the substance **lysozyme.** This is found throughout the natural world, in plants, animals, and molds, and in human body fluids such as tears, **mucus,** and saliva. Fleming saw that lysozyme could harm, kill, and dissolve various types of **bacteria.**

Fleming knew that bacteria are found everywhere—floating in air, on skin and clothes, in food and drink, on plants, and in the soil. He realized that all living things must be able to protect themselves from most of the harmful bacteria. Otherwise, the bacteria would be multiplying and threatening **infection** almost all the time.

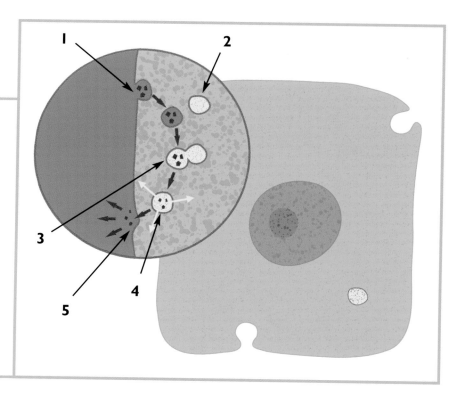

A living cell can take in, or "eat," bacteria (1). Inside the cell, tiny bag-like lysosomes (2) release natural digestive chemicals called lysozymes (3). These dissolve the bacteria (4), and the leftovers are ejected (5).

A natural defense

The natural chemical called lysozyme was part of this defense. Fleming showed that it was effective against many bacteria that caused minor infections. However, he found it was not effective against the really harmful and dangerous types of bacteria. This was partly to be expected. Bacteria that caused major infections could do so precisely because they were unaffected by lysozyme. Alec hoped to test more sources of lysozyme to find an unusually powerful version that would kill really harmful bacteria.

Fleming reported the results of his experiments at medical meetings, but few people took notice. As a public speaker, Alec was nervous, lacked confidence, and tended to mumble. His listeners became bored or turned their thoughts elsewhere. Further research showed that lysozyme was not as powerful as Alec had first thought, and gradually, he lost enthusiasm.

> **In Fleming's words:**
>
> When Alec first tested lysozyme, he was amazed at how it could dissolve bacteria: *"I put into a test tube a thick, milky **suspension** [tiny particles floating in liquid] of bacteria, added a drop of tear, and held the tube for a few seconds.... The contents became perfectly clear. I had never seen anything like it."*

A new house

In 1922, Alec and Sally moved to a larger house in London, at 20 Danvers Street. This was near the Chelsea Arts Club, and the Flemings became friends with more artists. Sally became interested in her Irish background. She decided that she now wanted to be called Sareen—a name that sounded more Irish to her. On March 17, 1924, she gave birth to a son, Robert. The Flemings' family life was very contented.

Fleming attended many social events, such as the Chelsea Arts Club Ball. This photograph was taken at the ball in 1926.

A Great Discovery

PENICILLIUM MOULD

FROM PROFESSOR ALEXANDER FLEMING 1935

Mold grew as a pale, fluffy covering on one of Fleming's round petri dishes. The substance it produced killed nearby small spotlike groups of bacteria. Fleming noticed this effect, leading to his great discovery.

In the late 1920s, Fleming's research at St. Mary's centered around how substances in human blood battled against **bacteria** and resisted disease. In July 1928, he received a great honor when he was appointed professor of **bacteriology.** Just a few weeks later, Fleming made a momentous discovery.

Alec went off to spend his summer break with his wife, Sareen, and son, Robert, at their country house, The Dhoon. But it seems that he had left some bacteria growing on **culture medium,** in petri dishes on the bench in his laboratory. He was interested in the way that the round patches, or **colonies,** each containing millions of bacteria, changed color as they grew. He wanted to find out if the colors showed that the bacteria were becoming more or less harmful.

HOW DID THE MOLD GET THERE?

There are many guesses about how a mold had appeared on the dish Alec had prepared for bacteria. Some say that Alec left the lid off the dish near an open window, and mold spores drifted in on the dusty London air, or that Alec sneezed over the dish as he was preparing it. Whatever the reason, Alec had the powers of observation to notice the effect of the mold and study it more closely.

In September, Alec was back in his laboratory. He had stacked many of the petri dishes for cleaning. But one of his former assistants, D. M. Pryce, came by, and Fleming gathered some of the dishes to show him. Fleming was suddenly struck by one of the dishes—it had not only bacteria, but also some type of mold growing on it. He put the dish aside to examine in more detail.

A brilliant observation

Alec had noticed that the dish had many round patches or colonies of bacteria on it, but around the area where the fluffier, lighter mold grew, the bacterial colonies were much smaller. Fleming reasoned that the mold might be producing some kind of substance that affected, harmed, or even killed the bacteria—the same hope he once had for **lysozyme.** The bacteria on the dish, *Staphylococcus,* caused sore throats, boils, and other **infections** of the skin and body surfaces.

New hope

Molds growing on dishes meant for bacteria were nothing new. Molds grow from **microscopic** seedlike structures called **spores.** Like bacteria, mold spores float in the air and get almost everywhere. Research workers take many precautions to keep them away, but spores still sometimes interfere with experiments, especially if the equipment used is not clean enough. Usually, Alec threw away moldy dishes, but he knew that this one might be different.

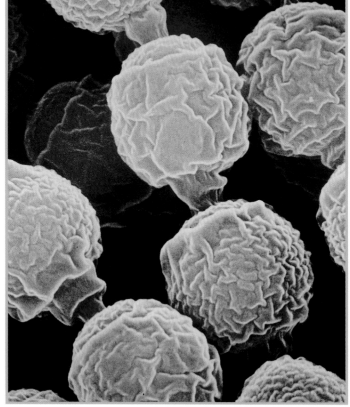

Tiny seedlike spores of molds, such as these **Penicillium** *spores, float in the air almost everywhere. They are far too small to see with the naked eye. In this photograph, they have been magnified over 10,000 times.*

Studying Penicillin

Alexander Fleming was proud of his ability to notice small things that might one day be important. He showed the moldy dish to his colleagues but they were not particularly excited. They were used to such sights after the "false start" of **lysozyme.** A colleague from another laboratory at St. Mary's identified the mold as a type of *Penicillium.* Its fluffy growths were common in soil and on rotting fruit. Alec took the name for the mold and changed it slightly to make a name for the mysterious germ-killing substance—**penicillin.**

Over the following months, Fleming grew the mold in flasks and tubes. He poured off the liquid part of the mold growth, which he called "mold juice," and tested it on various harmful **bacteria.** He was amazed to see that it was effective against many of them. It killed them—or at least stopped their growth.

Further experiments

Alec also tested as many other molds as he could find. This process involved him in a strange search for rotting fruit, old clothes, animal droppings, and dirt. Alec's colleagues worried about his state of mind. But none of these other molds had the same effect as the original *Penicillium* from the *Staphylococcus* dish.

Fleming's discovery had actually been a major piece of good luck. The mold on the lab dish just happened to be a natural strain of *Penicillium* with great bacteria-killing powers. If it had been a more ordinary, common strain of *Penicillium,* then the whole discovery may never have happened.

This Penicillium *mold grows on the surface of a rotting nectarine.*

A promising start

Fleming grew more *Penicillium* and filtered the "mold juice" to test it in various ways. It was important to show that penicillin was not only good at killing or disabling bacterial germs, but also that it was not toxic, or poisonous to people. Fleming injected the juice into animals. He washed the skin and eyes of human volunteers with it. He also mixed it with blood in test tubes, to see if it harmed the white blood cells called lymphocytes, that help the body's natural defenses against **infection.** He even used it on one of his assistants to treat an infection, washing it into his nose and sinuses. The tests pointed to powerful action against many dangerous bacteria, but few other harmful effects.

In Fleming's words:

Fleming became so excited about his penicillin "mold juice" that he carried it around to show people, even away from work. A colleague described how Alec and Sareen visited them one Sunday, and Alec pulled a slab-shaped glass container from his pocket. He showed the container to them with the words: *"From this slab will come things that will create worldwide interest."* However, the others present agreed that it was *"only a dirty slab."*

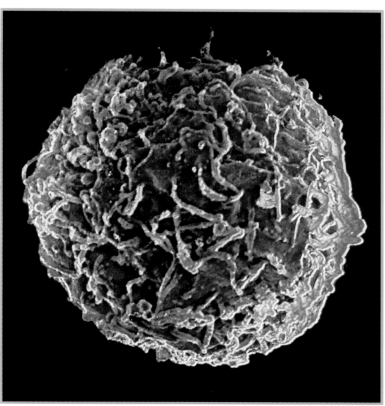

Microscopic blood cells such as this lymphocyte are part of the body's natural defense against bacteria. Penicillin did not affect these cells or interfere with the body's defenses.

Pure Penicillin?

Fleming continued his tests and experiments on **penicillin** into 1929. But he found it difficult to persuade anyone else that penicillin could be a new wonder drug. His boss, Almroth Wright, still believed that **vaccination** and similar methods to stimulate the body's natural defenses were the best way to proceed. For him, this was preferable to attacking **bacterial** germs with artificial drugs such as Salvarsan, or even substances obtained from living things, like penicillin.

After his main work on penicillin in 1928–30, Fleming continued his laboratory studies on a variety of other topics through the 1930s.

In 1929, Fleming presented his results to the **Medical Research Club,** a British organization that discusses drug research and other medical matters. As with **lysozyme,** there was little reaction or support from the audience. Again, this was partly due to Fleming's quiet and shy manner, and the way he announced his discovery.

The need for pure penicillin

Fleming needed to obtain penicillin in pure form to study its chemical composition, find out how powerful it was, and show that it was active against bacteria but harmless to people. Only then could penicillin be tested on real patients.

However, penicillin was difficult to purify from its yellowish mold juice. Suitable scientists for this work were chemists and biochemists, not **bacteriologists** like Fleming. One of his assistants, Stuart Craddock, teamed up with another colleague, Frederick Ridley, who had worked with Fleming on lysozyme. They tried all kinds of methods, but at some stage of the process, the penicillin's ability to kill bacteria suddenly and mysteriously vanished.

The name "antibiotic"

Fleming thought that penicillin might kill germs in the same way as **antiseptics,** by powerful chemical action. However, it worked more slowly than antiseptics, taking several hours rather than a few minutes. So he called it a slow-acting antiseptic. Then he began to use the name **"antibiotic."**

Other chemists and scientists tried to make pure penicillin from the mold juice, but with no success. Fleming still believed that penicillin could be a new "magic bullet" against **infection** by bacteria. But he had plenty of other work to do—not only research, but also running the department. St. Mary's Hospital was growing fast. In 1933, King George V opened the new medical school. Fleming was kept very busy.

ONGOING IMPACT ⟩ Antibiotics

The word antibiotic means "against life." It was made up in 1889 to describe substances that prevented living things from working properly, or that even killed them. The name is now used for the general group of drugs that includes penicillin and similar substances that work against **microbes**—chiefly against bacteria and similar germs, but not against **viruses.**

Modern drug researchers have many high-technology computerized aids, but they still use equipment such as microscopes, petri dishes, and test tubes, just as in Fleming's time.

The Wonder Drug at Last

During the 1930s, Fleming worked on a variety of research topics. These included more experiments on his **bacteria,** such as *Staphylococcus,* and on **vaccines, antiseptics, lysozyme, penicillin,** and treatments for illnesses such as influenza and **pneumonia.** In 1932, he became president of the **pathology** section of the **Royal Society of Medicine.** His home life was happy and settled, at Danvers Street during the week and at The Dhoon for weekends and vacations. Alec valued his relaxation time, and spent happy hours playing games with his son, Robert.

Another "magic bullet"

In 1932 in Wuppertal, Germany, scientist Gerhard Domagk discovered the second major "magic bullet" drug, Prontosil. It was a laboratory-made chemical that was already in wide use as a dye. When injected, it cured **infection** by *Streptococcus* bacteria. The news spread, and Fleming carried out some research on the so-called "sulfa drug," reporting his results in 1938–40.

Howard Florey was one of the scientists who succeeded in purifying penicillin.

Pure at last

Meanwhile, penicillin had at last come to the notice of other medical scientists. In 1936, German-born biochemist Ernst Boris Chain (1906–1979) came to Oxford University, in England to help Australian researcher Howard Florey (1898–1968) with his research on the lysozyme. The research had been going on since 1929. Chain and Florey eventually purified a version of lysozyme. They read scientific articles on lysozyme and other bacteria-killing substances, including penicillin. At this time, they were not aware of Fleming's role in its discovery, and Fleming was not aware of their work.

I. Quick freezing

Flask

Mold juice

Deep-frozen mold juice

Deep-freeze mix

2. Drying

To vacuum pump

Desiccant

Refrigerator

The vacuum freeze-drying method used to make pure penicillin has two stages.

In their search for possible new medical drugs, Florey and Chain recognized that penicillin could be important—as Fleming already knew. In 1940, after many long and complicated experiments, they finally succeeded in making pure penicillin from the "mold juice." This was partly due to their greater knowledge of the chemical processes that happen inside living things. It was also due to a new laboratory technique, called **vacuum freeze-drying,** that had only just been developed. Fleming briefly visited Florey and Chain at Oxford and took a mild interest in their work, but did not become closely involved in what they were doing.

In 1940, Florey, Chain, and their colleagues made enough pure penicillin to test on animals. They tried it on a few human patients in 1941–42. The results were amazing. Reports began to appear about yet another "wonder drug." But World War II had begun in 1939, and scientists were urged to help the war effort. Penicillin was a great hope for the future, but money and equipment to make larger quantities of it were very scarce.

A NEW TECHNIQUE

Vacuum freeze-drying is a method of removing unwanted substances from a mixture to leave a single pure substance as a solid. First, the liquid mixture is quick-frozen to a very low temperature, minus 58 °F (minus 50 °C) or less, by placing it in a special deep-freezer or freezing substance. Then the deep-frozen mixture is put into a container. The air inside is sucked out using a pump to create an airless atmosphere, or vacuum. The unwanted substances "dry" away into the vacuum. They turn into gases and are sucked out of the container. Water is absorbed by a drying agent in the container, called a desiccant. The desired substance is left as a pure solid.

35

A Great New Weapon

Fleming continued his work at St. Mary's as best he could in wartime London. His Danvers Street home was damaged by bombing, and he had to move to a colleague's house in Highgate. Sareen and Robert stayed with friends and family, away from the worst of the bombing.

Meanwhile, Florey and Chain were trying to raise interest and funds so that **penicillin** could be mass-produced. They were making small quantities at the Dunn School in Oxford where they worked, but not enough for proper patient tests. In 1941, Florey went to the United States and asked the government to set up a small "penicillin factory" at Peoria, Illinois, and then a larger one at the site of the Merck drug company in Rahway, New Jersey. Penicillin tests on patients continued with great success.

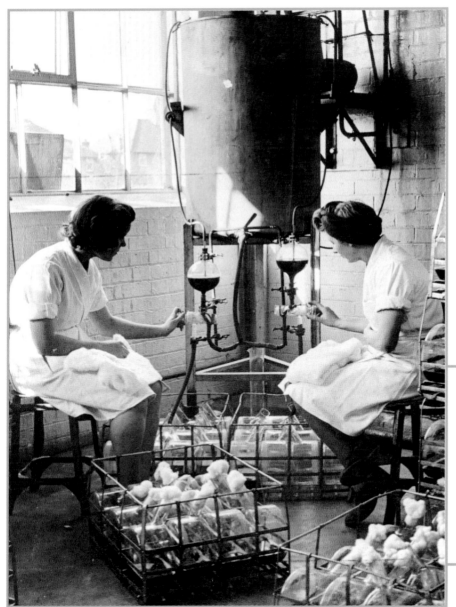

Penicillin "mold juice" was grown in large vats and purified for tests on patients, on a small scale in Oxford in 1941, and then in larger amounts in the United States.

From its first large-scale trials on troops in World War II, beginning in 1943, penicillin was a great success at preventing or treating infection.

A better mold

The method of growing **Penicillium** mold, like its discovery, owed something to chance and luck. **Corn-steep liquor** was made during the manufacture of large quantities of starch from corn crops. This substance proved ideal as a **culture medium** for growing the mold, just like a factory version of the test tubes in Fleming's laboratory thirteen years earlier. Florey and Chain also added their own improvements to the procedure. They even found another strain of the mold in a rotting melon that yielded more penicillin.

Another patient saved

Medical experts—and then the public—became aware of the huge success of penicillin. In early August 1942, Fleming himself, still largely unknown as the drug's discoverer, asked for supplies of penicillin. He wanted to treat a patient who worked for the optical company J. and R. Fleming, set up by his brothers. Again, the results were astonishing.

The newspapers began to print letters and stories about the latest wonder drug. But still the general public did not seem to know how penicillin had been discovered.

HELPING TO SAVE THE WAR

Mass production of penicillin began in earnest in the United States in 1943. Its first large-scale use was for soldiers in North Africa who had **infected** wounds in the hot, fly-infested conditions. It saved thousands of lives almost at once. Its use spread, and by the end of World War II, in 1945, it was the most effective life-saving drug in the world.

- In June 1943, enough penicillin was produced to treat 170 patients per month.
- In June 1944, this had risen to 40,000 patients each month.
- By June 1945, the rate was 250,000 patients every month.

Fame at Last

It was Alexander Fleming's boss who finally made sure that Alec was recognized as the discoverer of **penicillin.** On August 31, 1942, Sir Almroth Wright wrote to the *Times* of London, stating that the credit "...should be decreed to Professor Alexander Fleming of this laboratory. For he is the discoverer of penicillin and was the author also of the original suggestion that this substance might prove to have important applications in medicine." From that day on, the life of "Little Flem" would never be the same.

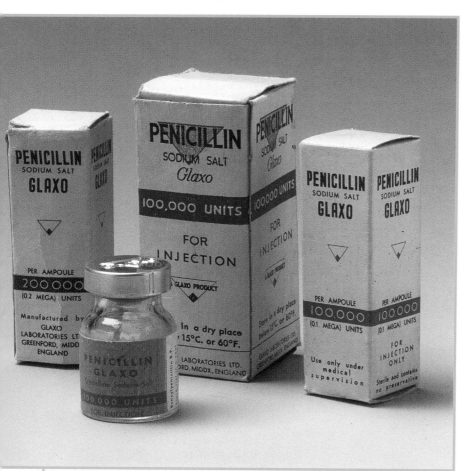

Penicillin was packaged in various forms and quantities, for use on different diseases and on patients of various ages. It could be injected or taken by mouth as tablets or capsules.

Penicillin's incredible success made the shy, reserved Alexander Fleming into a world champion. Suddenly, he was the subject of hundreds of newspaper stories, magazine articles, and radio and television programs. The extraordinary story of penicillin's discovery, and of Fleming's own career full of chance events, led to many myths. One such story said that Fleming had risen from a poverty-stricken childhood in darkest Scotland, where he walked barefoot for hours to school each day, to become a world-famous scientist who, alone, had discovered, purified, and tested penicillin almost with his bare hands.

Known around the globe

Fleming quietly accepted his part of the credit for the success of penicillin, but he was always careful to mention the work done by Florey, Chain, and other scientists and doctors. However, Florey, especially, was less eager to receive attention. Florey disliked personal publicity and distrusted journalists. Furthermore, the tale of how Fleming discovered penicillin was easier for people to understand than the complicated chemistry of Florey and Chain. So Fleming became the hero of the hour.

Fleming received many awards, honors, and titles in the years following penicillin's early success. He was elected a **Fellow** of the **Royal Society** in 1943, and was knighted as Sir Alexander Fleming in 1944. The honors rose to some 25 university degrees, 26 medals, 18 prizes, 13 decorations, and membership in 87 scientific organizations and academies. He also received the honor of being made a Freeman, or honored citizen, of Paddington in London, where St. Mary's Hospital is located. He also became a Freeman of Darvel in Scotland, and later of Chelsea, in the part of London where he lived.

In 1945, Fleming, Florey, and Chain jointly received the **Nobel prize** for physiology or medicine. This was, and still is, the leading global award for any scientist. Fleming had received an honor that most scientists can only dream of.

The Nobel prize medal awarded to Fleming on October 25, 1945, was great recognition for any scientist.

Great Man of Medical Science

From the mid-1940s, Alexander Fleming was busy with triumphant trips, tours, and visits all over the world. He had improved as a public speaker and was in great demand. Also around that time, other **antibiotics** appeared. In 1944, Russian-American scientist Selman Waksman (1888–1973) discovered **streptomycin,** produced by another type of **bacteria** called *Streptomyces.* This was the first drug treatment for **tuberculosis.**

In 1946, Alec was saddened when his longtime boss, friend, and occasional opponent Almroth Wright retired. He was even more upset when Wright died the following year, at age 85. Meanwhile, Fleming's own career rushed on. He became principal, or leader, of the Institute of **Pathology** in 1946, and continued to direct the Pathology and Research department at St. Mary's, which was renamed the Wright-Fleming Institute in 1947. Fleming also greatly valued another honor—the medal he received in September 1945 from the **Pasteur Institute** research center in France.

In mid–1949, Alec had the honor of meeting the pope at the Vatican in Rome, and U.S. President Truman at the White House in Washington, D.C. But later that same year, Sareen Fleming died after a fairly short illness. Alec, who was 68 years old at the time, was devastated. They had been a close and loving couple for nearly 34 years. Fleming became very withdrawn. His friends worried about his health and state of mind. But eventually, he threw himself back into his work, and also spent more time at the Chelsea Arts Club.

Fleming is carried by students at the University of Edinburgh, where he was appointed Lord Rector in 1951.

Alec and his second wife, Amalia, married on April 9, 1953, at the Chelsea Register Office. Typically shy and secretive, he told only one or two friends.

He was also helped by his many travels around the globe, and by a new, close friend at St. Mary's.

The later years

This new friend was Dr. Amalia Voureka, a Greek doctor who had come to St. Mary's in 1946 to work as a researcher. After Sareen's death, Amalia and Alec became very close, and they married in 1953.

Later that year, Alec suffered from **pneumonia**—but was cured with **penicillin.** He resigned as head of the Wright-Fleming Institute in 1955, but kept his own laboratory at St. Mary's to "potter about," as he put it. At the age of 73, he still went on tours around the world and seemed fit and active, so it was a surprise when he died suddenly of a heart problem on the morning of March 11, 1955.

Alexander Fleming was buried at St. Paul's Cathedral, London, alongside other great British heroes. He was remembered with national and international honors, and was mourned by millions as the man whose discovery saved their lives.

Fleming's Legacy

Countless people owe their lives to penicillin, one of most successful drugs and greatest medical advances the world has ever seen.

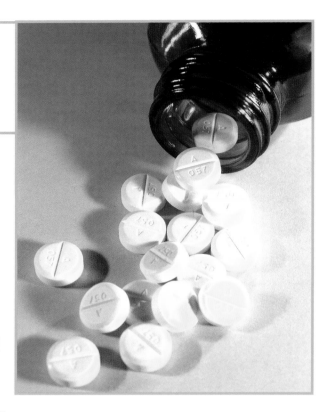

At Fleming's funeral, his old medical student friend C. A. Pannett said that Fleming, "by his work… has saved more lives and relieved more suffering than… perhaps… any man who has ever lived." The Alexander Fleming Laboratory Museum was opened in 1993 by St. Mary's Hospital Trust. Research continues today to find new and better **antibiotics.** It is a huge industry—based on Fleming's discovery of a moldy dish on a laboratory bench.

ONGOING IMPACT | Antibiotic resistance

In 1946, Fleming had suggested that some bacteria might become unaffected by antibiotics such as penicillin. The bacteria multiply and change so rapidly, every 15–20 minutes, that resistant types or strains appear. This happens especially if the antibiotic doses are too low or are given for too short a time. This has indeed happened, and new diseases now occur that are resistant to most antibiotics. There is a continuing need for new, better antibiotics, and for great care and caution in using them.

Luck, genius, or both?

But was Fleming really a brilliant medical scientist—or was he just lucky? Probably both. If he had not discovered **penicillin,** he would still be remembered as an outstanding expert on **bacteria** and other germs, and how to treat **infections** caused by them. If the moldy dish of 1928 had been seen by someone without Fleming's keen eyes, powers of observation, and great interest in odd events, then penicillin might never have been discovered. It is often said that success favors those with foresight. Would another research scientist have been so lucky?

After the success of penicillin, medical scientists began to test many similar molds or fungi, and other kinds of living things, in the search for powerful germ-killing substances. This work continues today. Modern researchers use incredibly accurate equipment. Computers design new drugs on screen, pharmacists make them in the lab, and **genetic engineering** methods can mass-produce them inside living things. The industry in medical drugs, or pharmaceuticals, is worth more than $450 billion each year.

Alexander Fleming's extraordinary discovery has had a huge impact on medicine. Through the use of antibiotics, medical treatment has greatly improved. Infections that would once have been life-threatening can now be treated more easily. Fleming's discovery of penicillin and the development of antibiotics is seen as one of the great medical advances of the last century. This wonder drug has saved the lives of literally millions of people. It is perhaps not surprising that Fleming has become a heroic figure in medical history.

*Celebrated in stained glass at St. James's Church in Paddington, Fleming is shown in his laboratory workroom, deep in study of his "beloved molds and **microbes.**"*

Timeline

1881	Alexander Fleming is born at Lochfield, in Ayrshire, Scotland.
1886	Fleming attends the local primary school, Loudoun Moor.
1891	Fleming moves on to school at Darvel.
1893	Fleming attends Kilmarnock Academy.
1895	Fleming leaves Scotland to live with his older half brother Tom in London. He attends Regent Street Polytechnic School.
1897	Fleming takes an office job at the America Line shipping offices.
1899	Outbreak of the Boer War in South Africa.
1901	Fleming studies for medical school entrance exams at London College of **Preceptors,** and enters St. Mary's Hospital Medical School as a medical student.
1903	Fleming's mother moves to London; he joins her and his brothers John and Robert to live in Ealing, West London.
1906	Fleming becomes a qualified doctor and joins the **Inoculation** Department of St. Mary's Hospital as a junior assistant.
1909	Fleming is elected a **Fellow** of the **Royal College of Surgeons** (FRCS). Paul Ehrlich discovers "magic bullet" drug called 606, or Salvarsan.
1914	Outbreak of World War I. Fleming works with an Army medical unit.
1915	Fleming marries Sally McElroy (also called Sarah and Sareen).
1918	World War I ends.
1919	Fleming becomes assistant director of the Inoculation Department.
1924	Son Robert is born.
1928	Fleming becomes professor of **bacteriology** at St. Mary's Hospital Medical School; also discovers **penicillin.**
1929	Fleming presents penicillin studies to **Medical Research Club.**
1936	Howard Florey and Ernst Boris Chain begin to work together to purify penicillin.
1939	Outbreak of World War II.
1940	Florey and Chain purify penicillin by **vacuum freeze-drying.** Penicillin is first tested on animals.
1941	Human tests of penicillin begin.
1942	Success of penicillin brings world recognition for Fleming.
1943	Penicillin goes into mass production in the United States.
1944	Fleming is knighted as Sir Alexander Fleming; receives several medals, honors, and memberships.

1945	World War II ends.
	Fleming receives many more honors, including sharing **Nobel prize** with Florey and Chain.
1946	Almroth Wright retires.
	Fleming becomes principal of the Institute of **Pathology;** makes several trips and tours around the world.
1947	Fleming becomes director of the Wright-Fleming Institute.
1948	Fleming is appointed professor emeritus of bacteriology at the University of London.
1949	Wife, Sareen (also called Sally or Sarah) Fleming dies.
1951	Fleming becomes Lord Rector of the University of Edinburgh. He continues to make trips and tours and receive awards and medals around the world.
1953	Fleming marries Amalia Voureka.
1955	Alexander Fleming dies at the age of 73.

More Books to Read

Gottfried, Ted. *Alexander Fleming: Discoverer of Penicillin.* Danbury, Conn.: Franklin Watts, Inc., 1997.

Kaye, Judith. *The Life of Alexander Fleming.* Brookfield, Conn.: Twenty-first Century Books, Inc., 1995.

Tames, Richard. *Penicillin: A Breakthrough in Medicine.* Chicago: Heinemann Library, 2000.

Glossary

antibiotic substance that kills or harms other living things

antiseptic substance used to clean a wound and make it free from germs

bacterium tiny and simple living thing that can be seen through a microscope

bacteriologist expert on bacteria, especially those that cause disease

colony small patch where millions of bacteria grow and multiply

corn-steep liquor liquid obtained from soaking corn

culture medium substance that provides food and a place to live for small, simple living things

fellow important member of certain public groups

gangrene disease in which body flesh rots away or decays

genetic engineering altering genes by scientific methods in the laboratory

infection illness caused when bacteria or other microbes get on to or into the body and multiply

inoculation giving a vaccine, usually by injection, to prevent a person from getting a certain disease in the future

lysozyme natural substance that can break apart or damage certain microbes

Medical Research Club British organization that discusses research into drugs and other medical matters

microbe microscopic living thing

microscopic too small to be seen except under a microscope

mucus slimy substance that protects body surfaces, such as the insides of the nose and throat

Nobel prize award offered each year for outstanding achievement in one of six fields: physics, chemistry, physiology or medicine, literature, economics, and promotion of world peace

oculist doctor who specializes in eye problems

Pasteur Institute scientific organization, based in Paris, that studies the causes and effects of disease, and microbes in general

pathology study of the effects of illness and disease on the body

penicillin natural substance, made by *Penicillium,* that works as an antibiotic

Penicillium type of fungus or mold that produces the antibiotic penicillin

phagocytosis when a microscopic living thing, such as a white cell in the blood, "eats" an item such as an invading bacterium

pneumonia severe disease of the lungs

preceptor person who teaches, instructs, or educates

rabies infectious disease, often caused by the bite of an infected animal, that is fatal if untreated

Rocky Mountain spotted fever infection marked by high fever, pain, and a skin rash

Royal College of Surgeons organization in London that works for progress in the detection of illness and disease, and treatment by surgery

Royal Institute of Medicine organization working for progress in the detection and treatment of illness and disease by various medical methods

Royal Society club set up in London in 1662 to promote research into the sciences

septicemia "blood poisoning," when microbes get into the blood, multiply, and spread around the body, causing serious illness

sexually transmitted disease illness or disease spread by sexual contact

smallpox severe illness causing fever, sores, scars, and sometimes death

spore tiny seedlike part produced by molds and similar living things, found in air, soil, and water

Staphylococcus type of ball-shaped bacteria that cause can skin boils, sore throats, and other problems

Streptomyces common type of bacterium that lives in the soil

streptomycin antibiotic substance produced by the *Streptomyces* bacterium

suspension tiny particles floating in a liquid

syphilis serious sexually transmitted disease caused by bacterial microbes

tetanus serious disease caused by infection with bacterial microbes that live in places associated with "dirt"

transfusion medical treatment involving blood or fluid being put into the body

tuberculosis infectious disease that can cause lesions and swellings

typhoid infectious fever, caused by bacteria, that produces a rash and irritation of the intestines

vaccine substance containing disease-causing microbes or their products, in dead or weakened form. They are put into the body by inoculation, preparing the body to protect itself against those microbes in the future.

vacuum freeze-drying process for obtaining a substance in pure form, done by freezing a mixture of substances solid, then gently warming it while in a vacuum, or airless place

virus microscopic agent that invades cells and causes infection

X-ray kind of invisible ray used to detect diseases or injuries inside the body

Index